SATURDAYS with Dad

SATURDAYS with Dad

NANCY AVEDIKIAN

1603 Capitol Ave., Suite 310 Cheyenne, Wyoming USA 82001
1-888-980-6523 | admin@urlinkpublishing.com

URLink Print and Media is committed to excellence in the publishing industry.

Book design copyright © 2021 by URLink Print and Media. All rights reserved.

Published in the United States of America

Library of Congress Control Number: 2021920656
ISBN 978-1-64753-993-1 (Paperback)
ISBN 978-1-64753-994-8 (Hardback)
ISBN 978-1-64753-995-5 (Digital)

29.09.21

Dedication

I dedicate this book to my dad who I miss
dearly but is now with the Lord.

Contents

Acknowledgements

I want to thank my husband and my family for encouraging me to write Saturdays With Dad. I also want to thank my dear friend Luz Cardenas for all her support in editing my original book, *Sábados con papá*, which was written in Spanish.

U. S. ARMY AIR FORCE

Sgt. Joseph Guarraia circa 1943

Prologue

———⟡———

What can I say about my dad—he was tall and handsome and always wore a thin mustache which he groomed every day. He was a hard worker as well as a strict disciplinarian, but who also had a good sense of humor. He was a drill sergeant in the Army Air Corps during WWII so he insisted on always having our house clean and in order.

I never realized how hard he had to work to provide for our family and to break free from the prejudice that immigrant families had to endure in those days. He succeeded in doing this in our community and won the respect of all who knew and worked with him. My dad, Giuseppe, who later changed his name to Joseph (Joe) was so proud to be an American!

My dad was the oldest of six siblings and grew up on 20 acres of land together with his uncle and aunt and all the cousins. During the Depression years money was tight and times were tough, but they managed to live a good life.

I learned so much about life from my dad and to this day I still miss him. You see I was only 14 years old when he died. For many years I was angry with God and couldn't understand why He would allow this tragedy in my life. As I grew older I realized that the Lord does allow these experiences in our lives so that we will come to Him and put our faith and trust in Him.

The Cider Mill

———⟨≈⟩———

"Hurry up, Nancy! Are you ready yet? What a gorgeous day this is. Let's go to the cider mill and spend the afternoon in the countryside."

It certainly **was** a gorgeous fall day and all the leaves on the trees were an explosion of color—yellow, orange, scarlet red, and every shade in between. The leaves appeared even brighter against the crystal clear blue sky. The colors reminded me of the oriental rug in my grandma's house.

"Yes, daddy," I called from the house. "Let me grab my jacket and a bottle of water."

Oh, how I couldn't wait for Saturdays so I could spend time with my dad! Today was just a perfect day to drive through the countryside and enjoy the scenery. And, it was a good day to buy some fresh apple cider.

As soon as I climbed into the front seat dad started the car and began to reminisce about his childhood.

"Remember, Nancy, when I was a boy I lived on a farm with lots of land around our house. I think that's why I love to drive through the countryside."

"Oh yes," I said as I thought that I'm about to hear a familiar story. But, that's okay because I love to hear these stories again and again. I think that this is the reason why I love Saturdays so much. He was able to relax and spend time with me. Weekdays he was busy working long hours and would come home so tired. But——-Saturdays were daddy/daughter days!

Driving along the winding road he began telling me his favorite story about his first day of school. "I was scared," he said. "I couldn't speak English. At home I heard my parents and the rest of the family speak mostly in Italian. We lived in a two-family house that my dad and his brother built. My family lived downstairs and my uncle and his family lived upstairs."

"But, daddy—how did you learn English?"

"Well, it took some time. But those first days of school were very interesting!"

"What happened?

"Well, the teacher asked me what my name was. I finally figured out what she was asking me."

"Oh, I guess that was the easy part, right?" I replied, as we both giggled!

"When I told her that my name was Giuseppe she started to write it with the letter 'J'. 'No, no', I cried. I did know how to spell my name, at least in Italian, so I tried to explain that it started with the letter 'G'. Oh my, then I really got mixed up and I knew that I was in trouble!"

I jumped in and added, "I think the teacher was getting mixed up too, right?"

Dad kept his eyes on the winding road while he finished his story. "When it was time for recess the teacher sent us outside to play and I sat alone eating my scrambled egg sandwich. I thought it was lunchtime so, boy, by the end of the school day, I was famished!"

"But just how **did** you learn English, Daddy?"

"Well, my older cousin, who lived on the farm with us used to give me 'English' lessons."

"English lessons?" I asked with a blank look on my face.

"That's right. He would sit me down at the table and get out some silverware. He pretended to be a professor and would say with a stern voice and a serious glance, 'This is a knife, this is a fork, and this is a spoon.' I kept thinking, man, I need to learn more than these words in order to function in school!"

We both burst out laughing! I heard this story so many times, but I always begged him to tell me the story again. I could tell that this was going to be a great day, just the two of us.

"Oh look, Nancy," he cried while we crossed the wooden bridge, "we're almost there!"

The small shop next to the apple orchard was so quaint. Bright orange pumpkins of all sizes as well as large pots of fall flowers lined the entrance. This Saturday there were crowds of people waiting to enter the store to buy all sorts of things; honey, fresh apples, and lots of fruit jelly. But most of all everyone came to buy fresh apple cider.

After parking the car we quickly got out to join the crowd. Dad took my hand as we got in line.

"Nancy, after we buy the cider," dad suggested, "I want to show you how they actually make the cider."

We walked over to a different building and when we entered I couldn't believe my eyes! There, in the middle of the room, stood an enormous vat that was the size of a swimming pool and was filled with crushed apples. Huge blades that looked like a fan swirled around and around, smashing the apples more and more with each turn. The smell was overpowering because the apples were fermenting. The attendant always offered free samples of cider and when we tasted it, I agreed with Dad that this was the best ever.

"Come on Nancy, let's go for a walk in the woods around the orchard."

The late afternoon sun shone brilliantly through the colored leaves, casting a heavenly glow.

"I'm going to pick up some of the leaves for my science project," I blurted out and ran off into the woods.

Dad shouted "Don't get lost—stay close by..." He never finished his sentence because I was already yards ahead of him.

'Wow,' I thought, 'there are so many different kinds of leaves! Boy, these will really make a cool notebook for my project!' I was so busy picking up leaves that I didn't realize that the sun was beginning to set. I turned around and...where was I and WHERE was my dad? Terror gripped me. Thoughts raced through my mind. Suppose there are wild animals out here! Oh, Nancy, why didn't you listen to your father? What was I going to do?

As I stood there sobbing in the middle of the forest suddenly I heard my name. "N – A – N – C -Y," shouted my dad! "I was looking all over for you! What happened?" Tears were streaming down my cheeks as I looked up and there he was! What a worried look he had on his face. He scooped me up in his arms and gave me a huge hug. Oh, what relief! "Come on, Nancy. I think we've had quite a day. Let's head home."

Do you know that it's the same with all of us? We try to run from God and think that we can make our own way. Finally, at the end of our struggling, we realize that we need help. We need the Lord Jesus. He loves us and wants to be our Heavenly Father.

The Bible says in John 1:12: "But as many as received him, to them gave he power to become the sons of God, even to them that believe on his name." KJV

Fall into the loving arms of Jesus and put your faith in Him. This is the most important decision you will make in your life.

The Italian Market

I woke up with a start because my thoughts were racing. 'Hey, isn't today Saturday? Wow, no school for me and no work for dad!' I jolted out of bed so fast that I nearly fell over while trying to get dressed. I ran down the hallway shouting, "Daddy, daddy what are we going to do today?" When I reached the back door I saw him in the driveway carefully washing the car as he always did on Saturday mornings. He shot a glance at me and stood there giggling with a smile on his face.

"Well, dear, I have a little excursion in mind for us today which I think you will really like!"

"Tell me, tell me!" I could hardly wait to hear where we were going.

"Today we are going into the city to the Italian market and bread store."

"Yay!" I shouted. My mouth started to water as I thought about all the delicious things we'll buy—salami, provolone cheese, sausage, and Italian bread. Oh, the bread is so good—crunchy on the outside and soft on the inside. It is so delicious with butter. But what I loved the most was the *cannoli*! This Sicilian pastry was a treat for us that dad only bought for holidays or special occasions. They are fried dough in the shape of a tube and filled with *ricotta* cheese mixed with whipped cream and pieces of dried fruits and chocolate chips. (Yum!)

"Tomorrow after church we'll go to your grandma and grandpa's house and have a big dinner," said dad.

There's sure to be enough food to feed an army. As always grandma will run around filling everyone's plate saying, *"mangia,*

mangia!" (eat up!) I really think that grandma's job in life is to feed everybody.

"Nancy, you're too skinny, *mangia, mangia,"* she would always say.

"But grandma, please, if I eat any more I'm going to pop!" But she never paid attention to me as she filled my plate again.

I snapped out of my daydream as dad called out, "Don't forget to straighten your room and make your bed before we leave." He always insisted that my brother and I keep our room neat and in order. He was a drill sergeant in WWII and he sure liked a clean house.

"And eat your breakfast before we go," he added. "Your mother fixed your favorite, scrambled eggs and cinnamon toast."

At last I climbed in the car next to him and we were on our way. We drove through our town and passed all the familiar streets. I saw where my other grandparents lived which was near my school. After a few minutes we came to the river that separated our town and the city of our destination.

When we crossed over the bridge dad said, "Oh look Nancy, there's the hospital where you and your brother were born. This is the town where I was born too. My parents came from Sicily and lived in an apartment here before they moved to the farm where I grew up.

I noticed that in this part of town most of the signs on the stores and shops all had Italian names. The city streets were narrow and crowded, not like the tree-lined street where we lived. After a while dad found an empty space to park the car. When we got out he said, "Hold my hand Nancy because there is a lot of traffic here. Oh look, there is the bread store."

When we entered the store a delicious aroma filled the air. Nothing like fresh baked bread! "Good morning Mr. Guarraia, good to see you again," said Mr. Lazzara who was the store owner. "How about some fresh baked bread today. I just took some out of the oven."

"Perfect. I'll take 5 loaves. We are going to have a family gathering after church tomorrow." Mr. Lazzara brought out the loaves and carefully placed them in the wax-paper bags that were printed with the name of his bakery. Dad continued chatting with him. I tugged on dad's jacket and whispered, "Don't forget the *cannoli!*"

Dad glanced at me and said, "Yes, Nancy! I know, I won't forget. I know they are your favorite. I'll let you choose the flavors you want, but remember they are for dessert tomorrow."

With sad eyes and a whisper I pleaded, "But can I just try one now? Please?"

"Okay, but just one," he said with a stern look and a wink. "Come on, let's hurry. We still have to shop at the Italian market." While we walked down the street I savored every bite of my treat.

Entering the Italian market definitely did not have the aroma of fresh baked bread like the bakery! Wow—what can I say about this place. You have to experience it for yourself! There was an odd mixture of odors: dried garlic cloves, dried onions, salami, and provolone cheese all of which were suspended on long cords and hanging from the rafters. However, the most distinct aroma was from the cages that lined the back wall behind the counter. Chickens, chickens, chickens—all cackling! What a racket they made. One of the hens looked straight at me as if to say, "Help me, help me—I'm not ready for the stew pot!"

"Dad, what are we going to buy here?"

"Well," he pondered as he stroked his mustache. "We need to get something for your school lunches." Then he turned to the storekeeper and said, "I'd like a pound of salami and a pound of provolone cheese."

"Certainly, Mr. Guarraia," and with great enthusiasm of a good salesman he grinned and added, "Can I interest you in a chicken for your Sunday dinner? See how plump they are? One will make a fine meal for your family."

Without a thought and with bulging eyes I met the gaze of that poor hen. She clucked and cackled at me seeming to ask for deliverance. "But daddy, who's going to kill it," I shrieked?

Thank goodness dad replied, "No thank you sir, we already have our meal planned." Whew! 'Poor chicken, you're safe for at least another day!' I thought.

Finally, with bags full of bread and groceries we walked back to our car. "Nancy, what did you think about our trip?"

"W-e-l-l," I slowly replied, "I loved the bakery, but I'm not too impressed with the Italian Market. All those live chickens made me nervous."

Dad burst out laughing and then we both cracked up! "Yeah, it's not like your typical American grocery store, right?"

On the drive home I dreamed about the fabulous dinner we'll have at grandma's house tomorrow. She'll fix *antipasto* (salad), spaghetti, and roasted lamb. When we are already bursting at the seams, she will bring out enormous trays of fruit and roasted nuts. AND, finally, my favorite dessert—*cannoli*! With full bellies all the men will tilt back their heads on the sofas and Uncle Giorgio will be the one to snore the loudest! Meanwhile, grandma and all the women will clean up the kitchen.

> *Did you know that the Lord is ready to serve a wonderful banquet to anyone and all who will come? The Bible tells us that Jesus said, "I am the bread of life: he that comes to me will never hunger; and he that believes in me will never thirst." John 6:35 (KJV)*

Christmas Presents

I always wanted to be a ballerina. Oh, to be able to spin and twirl on tippy toes in a beautiful costume that is covered in tiny pearls and colored sequins. I could imagine myself gliding across the stage and winning the applause of the audience. One of my classmates took ballet lessons from the time she was four years old. I must admit that I was a little jealous! In third grade I finally worked up the courage to ask my dad if I could take ballet lessons.

One Saturday while he was washing the car, I casually asked him, "Dad, do you think could I take ballet lessons?" Of course, I already knew what the answer would be, but it never hurts to ask!

Just like I expected he gave the same response I would always hear about saving money, "Honey, you know that dance lessons are expensive and we don't have extra money for things like that. Besides, that isn't something that is necessary."

I still remember the year before when we had a class play for the school and invited all our parents. Of course, my friend was chosen to play the part of the beautiful butterfly. She was fully adorned in a spectacular costume covered in tiny pearls and colored sequins that shot flashes of rainbow light with every twirl she made. Oh, how the audience would clap and cheer with every leap she performed. Meanwhile, the rest of us were located in the background in our simple and plain costumes. Well, at least I got to play the part of a flower and not a tree stump like some of the others!

Well, I had a plan! A few weeks before Christmas I began hinting to my parents that if I had ballet shoes, I could also use them as house slippers. I'm not sure they totally bought the idea but if I could convince my mom then she might talk to dad about this. Oh, if only I could own a pair of ballet shoes!

Ballet shoes, ballet shoes, that's all I could think about day and night and I was not about to give up on my dream! One day during math class the teacher called on me, "Nancy, if we add 16 and 52 what is the total?"

In an instant I popped out of my day dream and began to stutter and in a timid voice whispered, "Uh, uh, I, I don't know." The entire class burst out giggling and pointing fingers at me!

"That's enough, class," shouted the teacher! "Nancy, have you been paying attention?" What could I say to her—that I was dreaming of ballet shoes and a beautiful costume with pearls and colored sequins? And that I was the star of the next class play?

"Nancy, I am going to have to call your father and tell him that you need to pay more attention in class!"

Under my breath I cried, "Oh no, teacher! Please don't do that!"

My dad was very strict with my brother and me and expected us to behave in school and do our best. After all he was on the town's Board of Education and my mom was a teacher in my school. If she calls my dad, fat chance I will ever get ballet shoes!

That afternoon I slowly walked home from school totally discouraged. Every house I passed by had beautiful Christmas lights on and some had manger scenes. Mary, Joseph and Baby Jesus were surrounded by shepherds. How peaceful they all looked. If only my thoughts could be that peaceful. Then a thought popped into my head. Isn't it true that sometimes miracles happen at Christmas time? Well, boy I sure could use one!

So here it was Christmas Eve and the only thing on my mind was ballet shoes. As always we went to our grandparents' house. When we walked in there were greetings of *Buon Natale* and the wonderful aroma of spaghetti sauce. Grandma greeted me with a huge piece of *calamari* and said, "Come, Nancy, try this—it's so good and tastes just like a lamb chop!" No, grandma. Fried octopus does NOT taste like a lamb chop! Oh well, maybe there will be *cannoli* for dessert.

Late that night we returned home and when I walked down the hallway to our bedroom I glanced in the living room. There stood our lovely Christmas tree all decorated with lots of tinsel and blue lights, my dad's favorite color. A sadness still filled my heart. Did my teacher call my dad about me not paying attention in class, I wondered? I slowly changed into my pajamas and climbed into bed pulling the covers over my head. I could hear my brother's soft breathing, but I couldn't sleep. Just then I felt my dad's hand touch my forehead and give me a kiss. "Merry Christmas, honey. Sweet dreams!" he whispered.

In the wee hours of the morning while it was still dark I felt a gentle nudge. I heard my brother whisper, "Nancy, wake up! Don't you remember what day this is? Come on, let's go see the presents under the tree!" Presents? For me? Hang onto that dream, Nancy! Quietly, we tiptoed past our parents' bedroom and down the hallway to the living room. There under the tree were presents piled high that surrounded our small manger scene. We rummaged through them to look for our names. I spied one with my name on it. I didn't want to get my hopes up, but it was the size of a shoe box. Oh, surely not, could it be? With trembling fingers I carefully ripped the wrapping paper and opened the box. Inside were the beautiful, pink satin ballet shoes that I longed for!

I couldn't contain my excitement and immediately put them on and began dancing around the living room! When I twirled around, there stood my dad with a huge grin on his face. I ran to him and he gave me a smothering bear hug. With tears in my eyes I whispered in his ear, "Oh daddy, thank you so much! They are perfect!"

That afternoon we visited our grandparents' house again. When we entered there was another round of hugs and *Buon Natale* from all the relatives. Then we sat down at the long tables that were set up and enjoyed another feast!

After finishing the meal my Godmother called me, "Nancy, come on over, I have a gift for you." When I opened the package I discovered a set of lounging pajamas that resembled a ballet costume. This was fantastic! Who cares if it is not the real thing with pearls and colored sequins. I have ballet shoes and a costume to wear when I dance around my house and dream of being a prima ballerina!

Did you know that the Lord, is so happy to bless His children? The Bible says: "Delight yourself also in the Lord; and he shall give you the desires of your heart." Psalm 37:4 KJV

The Beach

I could tell when I woke up that this July day was going to be a real scorcher. It was already hot and humid. But wait—it's Saturday and last night dad promised to take us all to the beach today!

Ever since I could remember I absolutely loved playing in the sand and bouncing on the ocean waves. During the summer heat nothing was more refreshing and fun like playing in the water. There were days when my friends from the neighborhood and I would get together and I'd ask mom if we could run through the sprinkler on the front lawn. It was so much fun pretending that we were Olympic swimmers heading for the finish line.

Mom would shout from the house, "What is all that racket about? I hope you are not making muddy holes in the grass! Your dad won't be happy about that!"

"Oh, no, we are being careful! We're just having a good time!" Meanwhile the water from the sprinkler was icy cold and felt like tiny needles pricking our skin! Each run through the sprinkler produced more and more squeals of delight. Yeah, what fun that was. But today—a trip to the beach! Wow! That's like winning a gold medal!

Since I had my beach bag all packed and ready to go the night before, I ran to the kitchen to help mom fill the picnic basket. She always like to pack hard-boiled eggs, corn muffins, fresh peaches and a huge jug of lemonade. That will make a nice picnic lunch under the striped beach umbrella while we wiggle our toes in the hot sand.

"Nancy!" shouted my brother. "Don't forget your beach bag. Come on, hurry up. Dad is loading the car." The trunk was already stuffed to the brim with all our gear for the day so I threw my beach bag in the back seat.

"Okay, is everybody ready?" shouted dad.

"You bet!," we all replied as we climbed into the car. Mom sat in the front seat next to dad and my brother and I squeezed in the back.

"Hey Nancy," complained my brother. "Scoot over and don't hog the whole seat. And why didn't you put your beach bag in the trunk with the rest of our stuff?"

"Because," I slowly replied with a look of agitation, "I want to be ready as soon as we get there!"

"Good grief. This little sister of mine acts like such a baby!"

"Mommy, he called me a baby! I'm NOT a baby!"

"Okay, you two in the back, simmer down. It is a beautiful day and we are going to enjoy it, so let's not spoil it like this. Look out the window and admire the scenery," said mom trying to diffuse a full-blown squabble.

Enjoy the scenery, I thought. What scenery, we are riding through the city. How boring! "Daddy, are we there yet? I think I'm getting carsick!"

"No, sweetheart. It's a long drive to the beach," dad replied while he kept his eyes on the highway. "Why don't you take a little nap to pass the time?"

Just them I felt a poke in my side. "Come on sis, let's play the 'silent game.' We can't say a word or make a sound. The first one who does loses the game."

I thought sarcastically, 'what an honor my big brother wants to play a game with me, the baby.' So I said, "Yeah, sure."

"Ha ha ha—you lose! I win!" He laughed and stuck out his tongue at me.

"Mommy, mommy he tricked me!"

"Oh, good grief you both are giving me a headache." Mom added, "I think we all should play the silent game."

Yeah, I think they are all trying to keep me silent! It's not fair being the little sister. With a long sigh, I decided that maybe I should take a nap like dad suggested. I'll just close my eyes and dream about all the neat things we will do today.

First, we'll enjoy riding the waves on a blow-up canvas raft and then, after our lips are blue from the cold water, we'll sit in the sun and warm ourselves while we build sand castles. Late in the afternoon we'll walk on the boardwalk, buy some saltwater taffy, and play the carnival games. Oh, then there are the motor boats, the bumper cars, and the merry-go-round to ride. But my favorite ride is the Ferris wheel. I just love climbing higher and higher and reaching the top and being able to see everywhere. I was never scared because my dad had his arms tightly around me. I used to laugh because he had his eyes closed the entire time because he was deathly afraid of heights! But he always rode the Ferris wheel with me because he knew how much I loved it.

All of a sudden I heard dad shout, "I smell the sea air!" He always said this even when we were still on the highway. He just loved to hear me giggle and say, "Really, where, where is the beach, I don't see it yet!"

"Well, look—look ahead! We're here!"

Looking down the narrow street I could see ahead where the sky met the ocean. For me this was the highpoint of every summer! I rolled down the window to smell the fresh ocean air. At last we arrived!

We rode around for a couple of minutes looking for a parking space. As soon as he stopped, I swung the car door open and jumped out. I was so excited and couldn't help but jump up and down, "The beach, the beach!"

"Oh, Nancy, calm down!" said my brother while looking at me rolling his eyes around.

With a grin dad said, "Okay, everybody grab something to carry. We have to go to the bath houses so we can change into our swimsuits."

As quickly as we could we changed and walked to the beach trudging along in the hot sand carrying all our stuff. It was crowded but we finally found a spot just for us. Mom and my brother spread out the blanket and dad opened up the colorful beach umbrella and set it near the blanket.

As for me I could wait no longer! I ran ahead to the water's edge and dipped my feet in the salty and chilly seafoam with screams of delight. While I was splashing water over my arms and face I didn't see a huge wave come at me. It was so strong that it knocked me down and before I could cry for help I was already under water! I struggled to get up but the wave was carrying me back out to sea. I kept swallowing the salty water while this wave pushed me back toward the shore. I could see my dad sitting on the blanket and wanted to call out to him, but I couldn't even breath. I was terrified!

At the point of drowning, I felt my dad's strong arms lift me up and carry me back to the blanket. In the midst of my coughing up the salty water and sobbing, I could hear my dad say, "Nancy are you okay? Are you okay? Come, let's go eat some lunch and then you can play in the sand with your brother.

Did you know that the Lord is ready to help you in your time of need? The Bible says, "The Lord is my rock, and my fortress, and my deliverer; my God, my strength, in whom I will trust; Psalm 18:2a KJV

The Swing

When I was five years old my dad promised to make me a swing and a trapeze in our back yard. So, one Saturday we were off to the hardware store to buy all the supplies he needed to construct it.

"Wow! Daddy, look at all the tools and materials that they have here."

"Well, this certainly is the store where we can find what we need," he replied with a big grin.

"What are we going to buy?" I asked, tugging on his jacket.

"Let's see we need some rope—no," he hesitated. "Better yet would be a long metal chain. That should be a lot stronger. Of course we need something for the seat—maybe a piece of wood."

"Boy, daddy you think of everything," I marveled!

Then he added, "Yes, let's not forget to get the metal bar for the top so that we can hang the swing on it. It should fit nicely between the two oak trees in our back yard."

I just love swinging because it makes me feel like I am flying. At recess time at school I was the one who could swing the highest. I felt so free!

After paying for all of our purchases dad said, "Let's go Nancy. We've got some work ahead of us."

As soon as we got home, I bolted out of the car and couldn't wait to tell my mom that we were ready to start building my swing. "Mommy, mommy, look at all the things we bought!"

"Oh, that's nice, dear," she said as she walked back in the house. "Your dad is so good at making things and I know you'll be happy with your swing."

Dad had already begun to unload all the materials for this project and then he went to his shop to get his tools. "Daddy, daddy, can I help?" I was so excited and couldn't wait to try out my swing.

"Why don't you just watch me while I work," he replied. "I don't want you to get hurt." I was so proud of my dad and his ability to make things.

We had such a nice back yard and between the two tall oak trees he started to make my swing. In no time at all he finished the project. Standing back to admire his work he smoothed his mustache and said, "There you go, honey. Enjoy your new swing while I take all my tools back to the shop."

Immediately I ran to try it out. I sat on the seat, grabbing the chains as tightly as I could. I pushed my feet on the ground to start swinging. I pushed harder and harder and quickly I felt like my feet could touch the clouds. Faster, faster, higher and higher I could feel the breeze blowing through my hair. I closed my eyes and dreamed I was flying.

I don't know what happened, but I really WAS flying! I flipped over backwards and the next thing I knew I was flat on the ground! BAM! I felt my head hit a rock and boy did that hurt! I tried to get up but was so dizzy and it even seemed like the two oak trees were spinning too. Finally, after a minute or two, I sat up. I touched my head and felt an enormous bump starting to pop out. Oh boy, how am I going to explain this to my dad? Maybe he will get mad because I was careless and maybe he won't let me play on my swing any more!

Finally, I worked up the courage and carefully walked into the house keeping my head down. Maybe nobody will notice that I had a monstrous black and blue bump on my forehead. Nope! Dad was standing in the kitchen and when I passed by him he shouted, "Nancy! What happened to you?" Between sobs, partly because I was hurting and still dizzy, I explained my sad story of how I flipped over on the swing and was afraid to tell him. "Oh daddy, please don't scold me! I promise the next time I swing I'll be more careful."

"Nancy," he answered with compassion, "don't ever be afraid to tell me when you get hurt. Come, let's put some ice on that bump. Wow, it sure is a doozy!"

Do you know that it is the same with us? We should never be afraid to tell our Heavenly Father when we are hurt or scared. He loves us and cares about us. The Bible says, "Casting all your care upon him; for he cares for you." 1 Peter 5:7 KJV

The Typewriter

"Oh my goodness!" I cried as dad carried in a large and mysterious box. I was very curious to know what was inside. I wondered if it had something to do with the "office" that dad had finished working on last week. This "office" was a small corner of the new room that we added to the back of our house. He always wanted to have his own space where he could spread out his paperwork to pay the bills and such.

I ran over to him and peered inside the box. With a serious look I blurted out, "Dad, what is this?"

With much authority and a serious face he swung his arm up and declared, "THIS, my dear, is a typewriter! These were invented years ago to assist office workers in writing letters and recording their transactions. Nowadays all the modern offices have them and people even use them on a personal basis, too. And, as you can see," he declared with pride and enthusiasm, "now the Guarraias are the proud owners of one!"

I politely stared at him, trying to keep a straight face, while I was thinking, 'This is a new invention?' It certainly didn't look "new" to me. It was so heavy and very antiquated. Actually, it looked more like it belonged in a museum! Knowing my dad and his interest in saving money I'm sure he must have gotten it at a garage sale, or maybe even a second-hand store! Well, I didn't want to offend him because he was really excited about owning this "new invention"!

"Dad, do you think that I can use it too? I could do my book reports for school and even write some stories."

"You bet, Nancy! I bought this for the family and, of course, you can do some of your school work on it. Come on over here and I'll show you how to use it." There were rows of round disks that had a different letter of the alphabet on each disk. "First you put some paper in this roller. Then you strike the keys and it prints the letters on the paper." This was really cool, but I thought it would take a lot of practice to use it!

I always wanted to be a writer and I hoped that one day I would be a famous author. I used to read a lot of books and thought that I could get ideas for ways to write and express myself. I was thinking that by using this "new invention" it would be a lot faster to write out what I wanted to say, rather than doing it the old way using a pen and paper. So, no time like the present, I climbed into the special chair that dad bought for his desk. "Hey, I feel really important now. Let's see, what do I want to write about? Hum…"

Well, we've had a long winter and a lot of snow this year. The more I thought about it, this could be the beginning of a poem. Here it goes, "It's slushy, it's sloppy, it's wet and it's cold, I've had all the winter my patience can hold!" Well, that's a start. Over and over I repeated these phrases and then more thoughts came to my mind. Wow, this "new" typewriter sure makes it easier to write things down. It wasn't very long after that I finished my poem. Well, it sounds kinda' corny, but not too bad for a girl in the 8th grade.

"Dad, let me show you what I wrote. What do you think of it?"

"Well, Nancy, I think you should submit it to our town newspaper and have them print it."

"Really? Really? Do you think they would print it? Do you think anybody would be interested in reading it?" Dad always had confidence in me and encouraged me to try new things so I was overjoyed to think that I might really be an author!

"Here is the address of the newspaper," he said. "Type out your poem on a nice sheet of white paper and write a short note to go with it."

"Oh yes, I'm going to do it right now!" After carefully reading over the poem and the attached note, I folded the papers, put them in the envelope and wrote out the address of the newspaper's office. Then came the agonizing wait to hear a response from them.

One week went by, then another. 'Oh dear,' I thought. 'I've been rejected!' Oh well, at least I tried. Finally, three weeks later we received our town newspaper. I scoured through each page to look for my poem. There on the last page under the title, "Letters to the Editor" I found my poem! Wow! I couldn't believe my eyes! There it was in print for all to read. I was so proud of myself.

Did you know that the Lord wrote us a letter? Yes, it's the Holy Bible. In it we find all we need to know about life. The Bible gives us instructions on how to live a good life. We need to read the Bible every day and memorize its words. It will encourage us when we are sad or lonely, it will guide us in decisions we need to make, and most of all it tells the beautiful story of how God sent His Son, Jesus, to save us from our sins.

The Bible says, "Thy word is a lamp unto my feet and a light unto my path." Psalm 119:105 KJV

My Sickness

One night I woke up with such a sore throat! Boy, I could barely swallow and I felt like I was burning up. Since my brother went off to college I slept alone in our bedroom, and this night I felt so lonely. I kept tossing and turning trying to get comfortable, but it was impossible. I must have awakened my dad because I heard him tiptoe into my room. He whispered softly, "What's wrong, Nancy? Are you having a bad dream?"

"No dad," I tried to tell him with a raspy voice. I attempted to explain my problem, but the words just wouldn't come out of my mouth. It just hurt way too much to speak.

When he felt my forehead he said, "Oh my! You have a fever. First thing in the morning I'm going to call the doctor." He left the room and came back with a cold, wet cloth and placed it on my forehead. "Try to get some rest, honey."

The following day mom, dad, and I were headed to the doctor's office. As we entered and sat down in the waiting room, they began to talk about what was wrong with me. I was beginning to get scared and nervous. Just then the nurse walked in and announced, "You may follow me to the examining room. The doctor will see you in just a minute."

All kind of thoughts were swirling in my mind, 'Is this a serious condition? What are they going to do to me?' Just then Dr. Martin walked in and greeted my parents. He felt my neck under my chin and then adjusted his mirror and light that he had strapped to his head. He moved in closer to me. 'Whoa,' I thought! 'This reminds me of a scene in the science fiction movies I've seen where the aliens take over planet earth!'

"Open wide, Nancy, I need to check your throat." He started shaking his head and had a worried look on his face. "Well, Mr. and Mrs. Guarraia," he said with a stern voice, "it looks like Nancy has a serious infection in her tonsils. Isn't this the third time this year that this has happened?" He continued, "This time I am going to prescribe a new drug called penicillin which she needs to take for at least a week. When she is finished taking it, we need to remove her tonsils."

Yikes! When I heard that I nearly fell off the examining table! Oh dear, I was more scared and more nervous than ever.

On the trip home I tried not to listen to my parents discussing all the details of the operation and what would happen to me. I really wished I could talk to my grandma about this because I'm sure that she would talk them out of it! Being from the "old country" she would tell horror stories of people that had operations and never made it out of the hospital! Surely she could come up with some home remedies that would cure me! I could tell that my mom and dad were nervous too but they didn't want to worry me.

The day of the operation we all woke up really early so we could get to the hospital. I was not allowed to eat or drink anything so this made me carsick. Passing through the city I was remembering all the Saturday trips that dad and I took, going to the Italian bread store and the Italian market. Oh, how I was wishing that this was the reason for this trip!

When we checked in to the hospital's admitting office a matronly and stern-looking nurse said, "I'm sorry, sir, but you will have to wait out here. Parents are not allowed to accompany the patient upstairs. These are the hospital's rules!"

But my dad, thank God, was not intimidated by this and said to her, "I don't care what the hospital's rules are! I'm going to stay with my daughter!!"

The nurse's eyes, bulged out, and in a surprised look stammered, "Ah, well, I'll I talk to my superior."

My dad really was something! Even though I was 12 years old I was so thankful that I didn't have to wait alone until it was time for the surgery. A few minutes later another nurse escorted us to the waiting room for surgery patients. She helped me change my clothes and put on the hospital gown. Tell me, why do these things have to tie in the back? I was hoping that it wouldn't come undone and show my underwear! How embarrassing!

Then the nurse said, "Okay, young lady. I'm going to give you an injection that will help you relax. Don't worry about anything." Yeah, right, don't worry!

I brought some books to read while I was waiting in the hospital bed. What was I thinking? Nancy, you are really something. Hardly a minute later I started getting sleepy, just like the nurse said I would. I looked over in the corner of the room and there sat my dad watching me. He was making funny faces and trying to make me laugh. He kept pretending that he was falling asleep!

A short time later the nurse came back and said to me, "Okay, Nancy. It's time. Let's go to the operating room." We proceeded down the hallway to my destiny; the nurse on one side of the gurney and my dad, holding my hand, on the other side. "Don't worry, Nancy. Your mother and I will stay close by." Why did everyone keep telling me not to worry? Well, in my mind I repeated Psalm 23 that my mom taught me years ago. 'The Lord is my Shepherd, I shall not want........' I never finished it and fell fast asleep.

'Good grief!' I thought. 'What is that awful odor, like rubbing alcohol, and how did I end up on my stomach, face down? I didn't remember turning over.' My throat hurt worse than ever and I didn't dare try to swallow. I slowly opened one eye. Everything was blurry, but I saw my parents standing next to the bed. 'Well, that's good. I guess I'm still in the land of the living!' I thought.

"Nancy, the operation is over," I heard my dad say. "In a little while, after you rest a bit, we will take you home."

Oh yuk! During the ride home I was carsick again. This time worse than before. Not only from being hungry, but also from the taste of blood in my mouth.

But, it was so good to be home and crawl into my own bed! I was tired, worn out, and very thirsty. I thought how great it would be if I had some watermelon. Surely that would quench my thirst. There was no way I could talk, so my mom brought me my small slate with some chalk. She said, "Don't try to talk just write down what you need." I was so weak and could just write one word. "watermelon."

"Yes, Nancy," she responded, "but it's wintertime, there are no watermelons in the stores right now. How about some fruit sherbet?"

'Well,' I thought, 'nothing will quench my thirst like watermelon.' I must have drifted off to sleep because when I woke up I could hear my dad in the kitchen calling me, "Nancy, I have a surprise for you!"

I couldn't believe my eyes when he marched into my room with a big plate of the sweet and juicy fruit that I was craving—watermelon! I sipped up the juice and swallowed as best as I could. Then, I laid my weary head on the pillow and slept through the night.

I never did find out where my dad got that watermelon in the dead of winter, but like I said, he was extraordinary!

Did you know that you can have an extraordinary Heavenly Father? Just put your faith and trust in Jesus and He will take care of you! The Bible says in Hebrews 13:5b, "...for he said, I will never leave you, or forsake you." KJV

Clean Your Room!

Last night we celebrated my 8th grade graduation and I sat in my room reminiscing all the events that happened these last few weeks. Since my dad was on the Board of Education for our town he was chosen to hand out the diplomas during the graduation ceremony. That was an honor and he was extremely proud to do so! As he handed me my diploma, I could hear him softly speak my name.

One of our class activities the last few weeks of school was going to an amusement center that was a lot like the boardwalk that I loved so much when I was younger. I was really excited that they had an Olympic-sized swimming pool. My friends and I made sure to pack our swim suits and extra clothing that we might need. Of course, the morning of the trip was rainy and cold. Too bad! No matter I was still determined to enjoy the pool. My friends and I didn't stay in the water very long because we started to turn blue. It was so cold! This was not the fun activity I had planned.

The last two weeks of school we practiced for the graduation ceremony. It would be in the same auditorium that all our school plays were held. I had to smile as I remembered that 2nd grade play where my friend danced around as the beautiful butterfly on this same stage. Well, we had all grown up and now got to wear our graduation gowns this time; the boys in blue and the girls in white.

My thoughts were interrupted by my dad walking in my room. "Nancy, what are you doing?"

"Oh, I was just thinking about last night's graduation ceremony and thinking about next year when I enter high school."

Lovingly, he explained, "Don't worry, you will do fine. Your friends from school will be going with you. And, you will meet lots of new friends. In the past you have always gotten good grades in your studies and I have confidence that you will do well." Dad always encouraged me to do my best. "Just remember that you are entering a new phase in your life."

"I know, dad, but I'm still a little scared."

"That's normal to have those feelings. Well, I have an idea that might help you. Clean out your room and get rid of all the things that you don't need anymore. That will give you more space and it will help you focus on what lies ahead." 'Okay, dad, any excuse for me to clean out my room!'

"Okay, daddy, I'll try." As soon as I said this I reached under my bed and pulled out a box of mementos that I had been collecting over the years. "Hey, remember this, dad?" I said with a smile.

"What's that?" he replied.

As I opened this booklet, a flood of colored dust fell to the floor. Dad said, "My goodness! What is this?"

"Don't you remember the day we went out to the cider mill and I got lost? I was collecting colored leaves for my science project? I guess they got a little dried out over the years!"

"It sure looks that way, Nancy. You sure like to save things, don't you."

"Well, that was a special day for me and I wanted to remember it." I kept on rummaging through the box and found some seashells I had collected from our trips to the beach. "Remember the time that I nearly drowned when the wave knocked me over? Then you came and rescued me!"

"Oh, look, dad, here is a copy of the poem I wrote that was published in the newspaper." Then with much care and tears forming in my eyes I showed him my pink satin ballet slippers. Of course, they didn't fit me anymore, but they were the most precious of memories that I had. Dad knew what they meant to me and put his arm around me and gave me a gentle hug.

"You do have wonderful memories, Nancy, and this is a good thing. But we can't live in the past. There comes a time when you have to leave these things in the past so they don't hinder our moving forward to the future. Do you understand?"

I nodded my head and agreed that I needed to clean out my room and my mind and prepare for the next school year.

"Very good. Now I have something very important I want to tell you."

That's what the Bible tells us in Philippians 3:13b, 14 KJV "...but this one thing I do, forgetting those things which are behind, and reaching forth unto those things which are before, I press toward the mark for the prize of the high calling of God in Christ Jesus."

Good Bye Dad!

As we sat on my bed, I turned and looked at him. "What is it that you want to tell me? You look so serious."

"Well, Nancy, you know how sick I've been this past year."

I quickly interrupted him and said, "Sure, dad, but you are going to get better!" Just like everyone else in the family I repeated these words so many times that I started to believe them myself. But...in my heart I wondered.

"Nancy, remember what we were just talking about? Remember how I said that we can't live in the past? Remember how I said that we need to prepare for the future?"

Upon hearing these words my heart began to beat rapidly. "What are you trying to tell me?"

Slowly he began, "Do you believe in God," he asked?

"Of course, I do, Dad." I responded in a timid voice. I had a feeling of what he was about to say, but it was something I dreaded to hear!

He continued, "This illness I have is terminal. Do you understand what that means?"

These words fell like a ton of bricks on my heart! "No, no, no, dad this can't be!" I shouted.

He hugged me tight as he answered, "Yes, it's true. But I don't want you to worry, I know that I am going to Heaven."

This felt like a horrid dream and I was not listening to anything else he said. The thoughts of this last year were like a tornado whirling in my brain. I remembered the day that my Uncle Samuel drove me to the hospital in order to visit Dad after he had his operation. While we traveled through the city we passed by Lazzara's Bakery and the Italian market. So many pleasant memories flooded my mind that day as I remembered the Saturdays that I spent with my dad.

At last we arrived at the hospital, where just two years before I had my surgery to remove my tonsils. My dad stayed close to me and comforted me, but now I could not do the same for him! Uncle Sam parked the car on the street next to the hospital's window near my dad's room. "Look, Nancy, look up on the 3rd floor. There is your dad waving in the window."

I still remembered my dad describing how he felt the day after his surgery. "The nurse brought in a breakfast tray. Oh, the coffee smelled so good and gave me the will to live. I tried to take a sip but because of the pain and the stitches on my tongue, I could barely swallow! So, like a newly-hatched bird I let a few drops trickle down my throat." When he told me this it reminded me of how I felt when I had my tonsils removed. How I let that sweet and delicious watermelon juice trickle down my throat!

I sat in silence with dad's arms holding me all the while I reminisced.

Two months later the new school year began and I started 9th grade. During the day I was busy at school, but at night I couldn't forget the words that dad told me, how this disease is fatal. One night, as I was almost asleep, I felt his hand caress my forehead. "What's wrong, dad?"

"Nothing, honey, I was just praying."

As the weeks passed and Christmas came and went, dad got weaker and weaker. One day in February the doctor had a meeting with my mom. "Mrs. Guarraia, I know how difficult it is to care for your husband at home. I am recommending that we admit him to the hospital where he can receive the help that he needs."

So then when mom and I came home from school we would fix a meal and eat in silence. Later she went to the hospital to visit dad and I went next door to our neighbor's house to do my homework. My brother joined the Air Force and was not living with us anymore. Basically, I was alone many times and just looked after myself.

One night in May the dreaded phone call came. My dad had left this life and was now in Heaven with his Savior. Knowing that dad's time was near, my brother came home a few days before so he could see him and help mom.

The main memory that I have of the funeral was the abundance of flowers. Dad was so well known and respected in our town that so many friends showed their love in this way. Even the flag at town hall was lowered to half-staff.

During the funeral I never found the courage to look at my dad in his casket. While the entire congregation sang "The Old Rugged Cross," I choked on the words. The only thing I could do was quietly count the number of flowers that filled the funeral home.

And so it was that I was thrust into the future and forced to leave behind my childhood. A few years later I came to the realization that I had to make a decision to give my life to the Lord. For me it was a very dramatic and emotional experience.

The Lord has been so good to me and has given me the desires of my heart. As I reminisce on my adult life I truly believe that my dad's prayers for me were answered!

And what about you? Give your life to the Lord. It is the most important decision that you will ever make!

"For God so loved the world, that he gave his only begotten Son, that whosoever believes in him should not perish, but have everlasting life." John 3:16 KJV

Baby Nancy April 1948

Joe Guarraia 1952

Joe, Grace, Tom, Nancy June 1951

June 19, 1961

Lincoln School Graduation 1961

Nancy & Daddy 1956

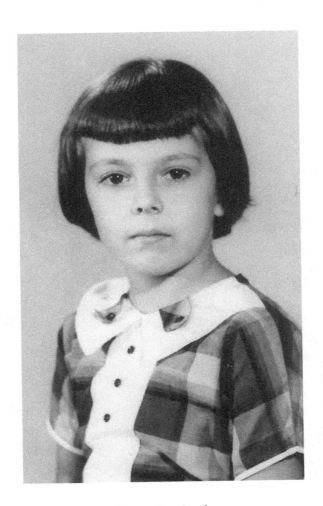

Nancy 1st Grade

Nancy's Swing Spring 1952

Ocean Grove

Palisades Park Fun House

Tom & Nan Circa 1952

The author in 2016